The Tempest

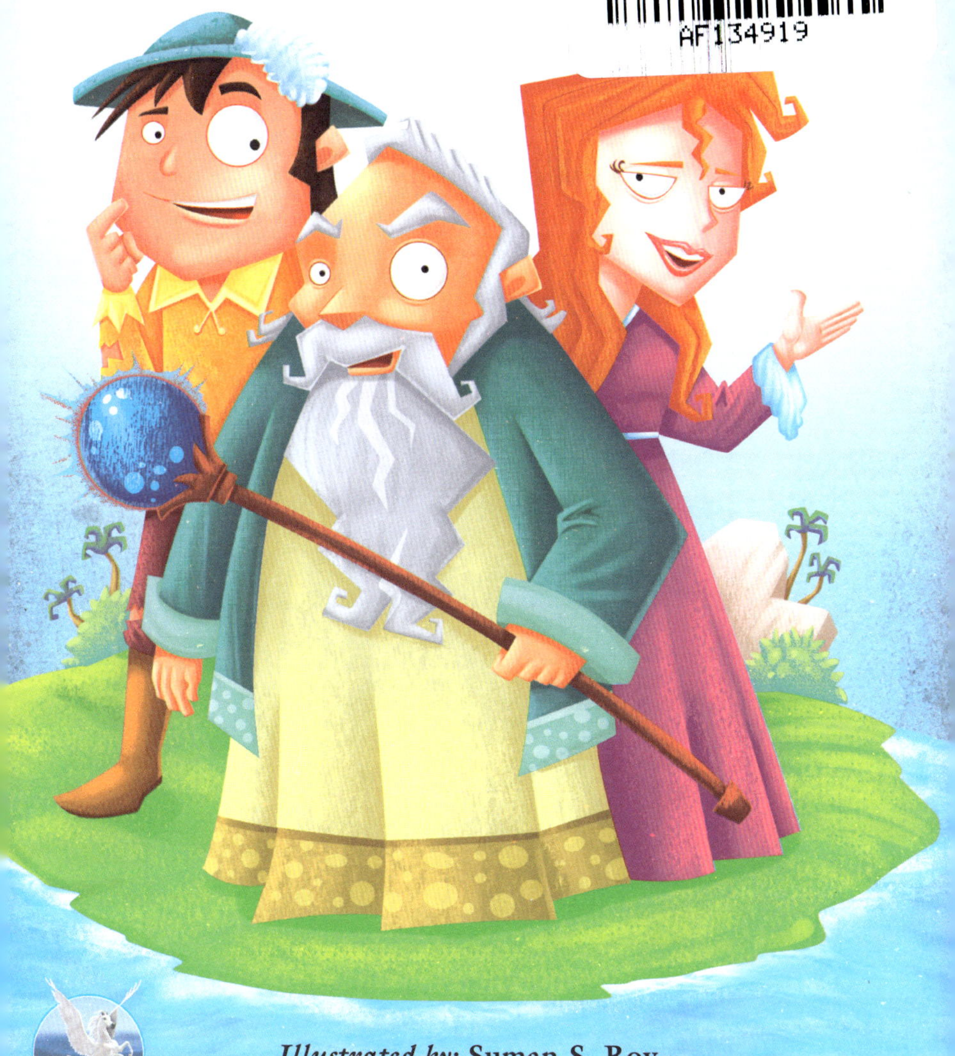

Illustrated by: Suman S. Roy
Compiled and Edited by: Tapasi De

Contents

1. The Tempest at a Glance   3

2. Who's Who in the Play   5

3. The Tempest   8

4. Post-reading Activities   36

5. About the Author   45

The Tempest at a Glance

The Tempest has often described by critics as a *tragicomedy* as both the elements of tragedy and comedy surface in it. It is one of the most enjoyble creations of Shakespeare.

Drama basically can be divided into three genres—comedy, tragedy and satire. Any humourous discourse which amuses and evokes laughter can be called a comedy. And a *tragedy* is a play that is based on human sufferings. In the 19th century, some critics identified some

Glossary
Tragicomedy a play or novel having elements of both a comedy and a tragedy
Genre Kinds of art

of Shakespeare's plays as containing elements of both tragedy and comedy. They named these plays as *Tragicomedies*. *The Tempest* is one such play which contains comic and tragic elements woven in the same plot.

Who's Who in the Play

Prospero

Prospero is the usurped Duke of Milan and the father of Miranda. He is also a powerful magician. The pursuit of knowledge gets Prospero into trouble.

Miranda

Miranda, the beautiful daughter of Prospero is a gentle and compassionate teenage girl. She is meek and emotional in nature.

Glossary
Usurp take a position of power illegally or forcibly

Caliban

Caliban is the son of a witch named Sycorax and the only real native of the island. He is the dark, earthy slave of Prospero.

Ariel

Ariel is an airy spirit and the helper of Prospero. He serves Prospero with his magical powers in many ways. He is mischievous and omnipresent.

Ferdinand

Ferdinand is the son and heir of Alonso, King of Naples. Ferdinand seems in quite a few ways to be as pure and simple as Miranda.

Glossary
Mischievous causing anger by playful tricks

Alonso

Alonso is the King of Naples and the father of Ferdinand. Alonso assisted Antonio in overthrowing Prospero.

Antonio

Antonio is Prospero's treacherous younger brother and the current Duke of Milan. He is extremely power-hungry and ruthless.

Gonzalo

Gonzalo is an old and honest lord who helps Prospero and Miranda to escape after Antonio usurped Prospero's title.

Glossary
Treacherous deceptive and unreliable

The Tempest

Long ago, there was an island in the sea, the only inhabitants of which were an old man, whose name was Prospero, and his daughter Miranda, a very beautiful young lady. Miranda came to this island when she was very young. And so, she had no memory of having seen any other human face other than her father's.

They lived in a cave made out of a rock and it was divided into several apartments, one of which Prospero called his study. In the study, he kept his books, which chiefly were of magic the knowledge of which he found very useful to him. This was because the island where he was thrown by a strange chance had been enchanted

Glossary
Inhabitants a person or animal that lives in a particular place
Enchant to fill someone with great delight or charm

by a witch called Sycorax, who had died shortly before his arrival. Prospero, by virtue of his art, released many

good spirits that Sycorax had imprisoned in the bodies of large trees, because they had refused to execute her wicked commands. These gentle spirits were always following Prospero ready to abide by his will. Of these, Ariel was the chief.

The lively little sprite Ariel had nothing mischievous in his nature. But even then he took too much pleasure in tormenting an ugly monster called Caliban, because he was the son of his old enemy Sycorax. Prospero found Caliban in the woods. Caliban was a strange looking creature, far less human in form than an ape. He took him home to his cell and taught him to speak. Prospero would have been very kind to him, but the bad nature which Caliban inherited from his mother Sycorax, would not let him learn anything good or useful. Therefore, he was employed like a slave, to fetch wood, and do the most laborious jobs. Ariel had the charge of making him do these services.

When Caliban was lazy and neglected his work, Ariel (who was invisible to all eyes but Prospero's) would come quietly and pinch him, and sometimes tumble him down in the swamp. And then Ariel, like an ape, would make faces at him. Then swiftly changing his

Glossary
Tormenting having severe pain or suffering
Inherited to receive property by the laws of inheritance

came to this cave? I think you cannot for you were not then three years of age.'

'Certainly I can, father,' replied Miranda.

'By what?' asked Prospero; 'by any other house or person? Tell me what you can remember, my child.'

Miranda said, 'It seems to me like the recollection of a dream. But had I not once four or five women who attended upon me?'

Prospero answered, 'You had many more. How is it that this memory still lives in your mind? Do you remember how you came here?'

'No, father,' replied Miranda, 'I remember nothing more.'

'Twelve years ago, Miranda,' continued Prospero, 'I was Duke of Milan, and you were a princess, and my only heir. I had a younger brother, whose name was Antonio, to whom I entrusted everything. And as I was fond of deep study. I commonly left the management of my state affairs to your uncle, my brother. I, neglecting all worldly affairs buried among my books, dedicated my whole time to the bettering of

Glossary
Entrusted to give or assign some responsibility
Dedicate to devote time or effort

my mind. My brother Antonio being thus in possession of my power, began to think himself to be the duke. The opportunity I gave him of making himself popular among my subjects awakened in him a proud ambition to take my place as the Duke of Milan. This he soon made true with the aid of the King of Naples, a powerful prince, who was my enemy.'

'Why did they not destroy us that very hour father?'

'My child,' answered her father, 'they dare not, so dear was the love that my people had for me. Antonio carried us on board a ship, and when we were some distance out at sea, he forced us into a small boat, without either a tackle, sail, or a mast. He left us there, as he thought that we would perish. But a kind lord of my court called Gonzalo, who loved me, had privately placed in the boat, water, provisions, clothes, and some books which I prized above my dukedom.'

'O my father,' said Miranda, 'what a trouble must I have been to you then!'

'No, my love,' said Prospero, 'you were a little cherub that did preserve me. Your innocent smiles made me fight against my misfortunes. Our food lasted till we landed on this desert island. Since then, my chief delight has been in teaching you, Miranda, and you have well profited by my instructions.'

'Heaven thank you, my dear father,' said Miranda 'Now please tell me, your reason for raising this sea-storm?'

'Listen to me then,' said her father, 'that by means of this storm, my enemies, the King of Naples and my cruel brother will be cast ashore upon this island.'

Having said so, Prospero gently touched his daughter with his magic wand, and she fell fast asleep. Just then,

Glossary
Misfortune ill fate or bad luck

the spirit Ariel presented himself before his master to give an account of the tempest, and how he had disposed of the ship's travellers. The spirits were always invisible to Miranda as Prospero did not want that she should hear him holding a conversation with the empty air.

'Well, my brave spirit,' said Prospero to Ariel, 'how have you performed your task?'

Ariel gave a lively description of the storm, and of the terrors of the mariners. He told how the King's son, Ferdinand was the first who leaped into the sea and how his father thought that his dear son was swallowed up by the waves and lost.

'But he is safe,' said Ariel, 'in a corner of the isle, sitting with his arms folded, sadly lamenting the loss of the King, his father, whom he thinks to be drowned. Not a hair of his head is injured, and his princely garments, though drenched in the sea-waves, look fresher than before.'

'That's my Ariel,' said Prospero, happily. 'Bring him here. My daughter must see this young prince. Where are the King and my brother?'

Glossary
Invisible something that cannot be seen with eyes
Drenched to get wet all over

'I left them,' answered Ariel, 'searching for Ferdinand, whom they have little hopes of finding, thinking they saw him perish. Of the ship's crew not one is missing though each one thinks himself to be the only one saved! And the ship, though invisible to them, is safe in the harbour.'

'Ariel,' said Prospero, 'your work is faithfully performed. But there is more work yet.'

'Is there more work?' said Ariel. 'Let me remind you, master, that you have promised me my liberty. Please remember that I have done you worthy service, told you no lies, made no mistakes, served you without grudge or grumbling.'

'Now, now!' said Prospero. 'You do not remember what a trouble I freed you from. Have you forgotten the wicked witch Sycorax, who with age and envy was almost bent double? Where was she born?'

'Sir, in Algiers,' said Ariel.

'O was she so?' said Prospero. 'I must remind what you have been through, which I find you do not remember. This bad witch, Sycorax, for her witchcrafts, was banished from Algiers and left by the sailors on the island. And because you were a spirit too delicate to carry her wicked commands, she shut you up in a tree, where I found you howling. Remember, I did free you from such a trouble.'

'Pardon me, dear master,' said Ariel, ashamed to seem ungrateful. 'I will obey your commands.'

Glossary
Grumbling to mutter when unhappy about something
Banished to be removed from one's land

'Do so,' said Prospero, 'and I will set you free.' He then gave orders what further he would have him do. And away went Ariel, first to where he had left Ferdinand, and found him still sitting on the grass in the same sad posture.

'O my young gentleman,' said Ariel, when he saw him, 'I will soon move you. You must be brought, I find, for the Lady Miranda to have a sight of your pretty person. Come, sir, follow me.'

Ferdinand followed in amazement the sound of Ariel's voice, till it led him to Prospero and Miranda, who were sitting under the shade of a large tree. Now Miranda had never seen a man before, except her own father.

'Miranda,' said Prospero, 'tell me what you are looking at there.'

'O father,' said Miranda, in a strange surprise, 'surely that is a spirit. O father! How it looks about! Believe me, father, it is a beautiful creature. Is it not a spirit?'

'No, girl,' answered her father. 'It eats and sleeps and has senses such as we have. This young man you see was in the ship. He is somewhat changed in appearance due to sadness, or else you would have called him a handsome person. He has lost his companions, and is wandering about to find them.'

Miranda, who thought all men had grave faces and grey beards like her father, was delighted with the

appearance of this beautiful young prince. And Ferdinand, seeing such a lovely lady in the deserted island, thought that he was upon an enchanted island, and that Miranda was the Goddess of the place. And so, he began to address her in that manner.

'I am sure that you are the Goddess of this island you beautiful lady,' said Ferdinand. Hearing this Miranda timidly answered that she was no Goddess, but a simple maiden. And as she was going to give him an account of herself, Prospero interrupted her. He was very pleased to find that they admired each other, for he plainly perceived that they had fallen in love at first sight. But in order to test Ferdinand's constancy, he resolved to throw some difficulties in their way.

So, advancing forward, he addressed Ferdinand with some severity and told him, 'Young man, you have come to this island as a spy to take it from me who is the lord of it. Follow me! I will tie you neck and feet together. You shall drink sea-water, eat shells, withered roots and husks of acorns.'

'No,' said Ferdinand, 'I will resist such a punishment until I see a more powerful enemy!' Saying this, he drew his sword but Prospero, waving his magic wand,

Glossary
Interrupted to stop something in between

fixed him to the spot where he stood, so that he had no had no power to move.

Miranda pleaded her father, saying, 'Why are you so ungentle? Have pity, father! I will be his surety. This is the second man I ever saw, and to me he seems a true one.'

'Silence,' said Prospero. 'One word more and you will be scolded girl! You think there are no more such fine men, having seen only him and Caliban. I tell you, foolish girl, most men are better than him, as he is better than Caliban.' This he said to test his daughter's constancy and she replied, 'My affections are very humble. I have no wish to see a better man.'

'Come on, young man,' said Prospero to the prince; 'you have no power to disobey me.'

'I have not indeed,' answered Ferdinand; and not knowing that it was by magic he was deprived of all power of resistance, he was astonished to find himself so strangely obeying Prospero. He looked for Miranda as he could not see her, and as he went after Prospero into the cave he said, 'My spirits are all bound up as if

Glossary
Constancy the trait of being faithful
Resistance the refusal to accept something

I were in a dream. But this man's threats would seem less of a burden to me if from my prison I would once a day see this beautiful lady!'

Prospero kept Ferdinand not long confined within the cell. He soon brought out his prisoner, and gave him a severe task to perform. He made sure that his daughter would know about the hard labour he had imposed on him, and then pretending to go into his study, he secretly watched them both.

Prospero had commanded Ferdinand to pile up some heavy logs of wood. Being a Kings' son, he was not much used to laborious work. Miranda soon found that her lover was almost dying with fatigue.

'Alas!' said she, 'do not work so hard; my father is at his studies. He will be there for three hours; please rest for a while.'

'O my dear lady,' said Ferdinand, 'I dare not. I must finish my task before I take my rest.'

'If you will sit down for a while,' said Miranda, 'I will carry your logs in that time.' But this Ferdinand would by no means agree to. Instead of a help Miranda became a hindrance, for they began a long

Glossary
Laborious something that requires effort and hardwork
Hindrance a thing that provides resistance or acts as an obstacle

conversation, and the business of log-carrying went on very slowly.

Prospero, who had commanded Ferdinand to do this task merely as a trial of his love, was not reading his books, as his daughter thought but was standing by them invisible, to overhear whatever they said. Ferdinand asked her name, 'Sweet lady, what is your name?' To this Miranda replied not forgetting to mention that this she had done against her father's wishes.

Prospero only smiled at this first instance of his daughter's disobedience. This was because he by his magic art had caused his daughter to fall in love so suddenly that he was not angry that she showed her love by forgetting to obey his commands. And he listened happily to a long speech of Ferdinand, in which he professed to love Miranda deeply.

In answer to Ferdinand's praises of her beauty, which he said exceeded all the women in the world, she replied, 'I do not remember the face of any woman, nor have I seen any more men than you, my good friend, and my dear father. How the features of women differ, I do not know. But believe me, sir, I would not

Glossary
Disobedience failure or refusal to obey rules of an authority

wish for any companion in the world other than you. But, sir, I fear I talk to you too freely, and I forget my father's command.'

At this Prospero smiled, and nodded his head and said to himself, 'This is going on exactly as I wished! My girl will be the Queen of Naples.'

And then Ferdinand, in another fine long speech told the innocent Miranda that he was heir to the crown of Naples, and that she should be his Queen.

'Ah! Sir,' said she, 'I am your wife if you will marry me.'

Just then, Prospero appeared before them. 'Fear nothing, my child,' said he. 'I have overheard and approved of all you have said. And, Ferdinand, if I have too severely used you, I will reward you by giving you my daughter. All your troubles were but trials of your love, and you have nobly stood the test. Then as my gift, take my daughter who is above all praise.'

He then left them alone so that they would sit down and talk together till he returned. Hearing this, both the lovers seemed more than happy.

When Prospero left them, he called his spirit **Ariel**, who quickly appeared before him, eager to relate what he had done with Prospero's brother and the King of Naples. Ariel said that he had left them almost out of their senses with fear, at the strange things he had caused them to see and hear. When they were fatigued with wandering about, and famished for want of food, he had suddenly set before them a delicious banquet. And then, just as they were going to eat, he appeared before them in the shape of a voracious monster with wings! The feast also vanished away. Then, to their utter amazement, this seeming monster spoke to them, reminding them of their cruelty in driving Prospero from his dukedom, and leaving him and his infant daughter to perish in the sea. He also mentioned that they were facing all these troubles as these were the punishments imposed on them for their misdeeds.

The King of Naples and Antonio, Prospero's brother, repented the injustice they had done to Prospero.

'We have indeed done injustice to Prospero and his little daughter. But now can we alter our actions after so many years?' they asked repentantly.

Ariel told his master that he was certain that their

Glossary
Voracious devouring great quantities of food
Misdeed a wicked or wrong deed
Injustice lack of fairness

penitence was sincere.

'Then bring them here, Ariel,' said Prospero. 'If you feel pity for them in spite of being a spirit, then won't I feel pity being a human being? Bring them quickly to me my dainty Ariel.'

Ariel soon returned with the King, Antonio, and old Gonzalo in their train, who had followed him, wondering at the wild music he played in the air to draw them on to his master's presence. This Gonzalo was the same man who had kindly provided Prospero formerly with books and provisions, when his wicked brother had left him to perish in an open boat in the sea.

Grief and terror had so stupefied their senses, that they did not recognize Prospero. He first appeared to the good old Gonzalo, calling him the preserver of his life. His brother and the King knew at once that he was the injured Prospero. Antonio with tears, and sad words of sorrow and true repentance, asked for his brother's forgiveness.

'Forgive me o brother for my thoughtless actions and excessive greed,' said he.

Glossary
Dainty delicate
Preserver one who protects
Repentance to feel sorry about some misdeed

And the King too expressed his sincere remorse for having assisted Antonio to depose him. Prospero forgave them. He said to the King of Naples, 'I have

a gift in store for you too!' And then, opening a door, showed him his son Ferdinand playing chess with Miranda.

Nothing could exceed the joy of the father and the son at this unexpected meeting, for each thought the other had drowned in the storm.

'O wonder!' said Miranda, 'what noble creatures these are! It must surely be a brave world that has such people in it.'

The King of Naples was almost as much astonished at the beauty and excellent graces of the young Miranda as his son had been.

'Who is this pretty maiden?' he asked. 'She seems to be the Goddess who has parted us, and brought us thus together.

'No, father,' answered Ferdinand, smiling to find his father had fallen into the same mistake that he had done when he first saw Miranda. 'She is a mortal but by immortal Providence she is mine! I chose her when I could not ask you, my father, for your consent, not thinking you were alive. She is the daughter of

Glossary
Immortal living forever

Prospero, who is the famous Duke of Milan, of whose renown I have heard so much. It is due to him that I have received a new life! He has made himself a second father of mine by giving me this dear lady.'

'Then I must be her father,' said the King; 'but oh! How odd will it sound, that I must ask my child forgiveness.'

'No more of that,' said Prospero. 'Let us not remember our past troubles, since they have so happily ended.'

And then, Prospero embraced his brother, and again assured him of his forgiveness. He also said that a wise overruling destiny had devised that he should be driven from his poor dukedom of Milan, so that his daughter might inherit the crown of Naples. Due to this divine providence, they had met in this desert island, and that the King's son had loved Miranda. These kind words which Prospero spoke to comfort his brother, filled Antonio with so much shame and remorse that he wept and was unable to speak. And the kind old Gonzalo wept to see this joyful reconciliation, and prayed for blessings on the young couple.

Glossary
Providence a territory

Prospero now told them that their ship was safe in the harbour, and the sailors all on board. He also told them that he and his daughter would accompany them home the next morning.

'Meanwhile,' he said, 'please accept some refreshments that my poor cave offers and as your evening's entertainment. I will relate the history of my life from my first landing in this desert island.'

He then called for Caliban to prepare some food, and set the cave in order. The company was astonished at the savage appearance of this ugly monster, who Prospero told them was the only attendant he had to depend upon.

Before Prospero left the island, he dismissed Ariel from his service, to the great joy of that lively little spirit who had always been a faithful servant to his master. Ariel was always longing to enjoy his free liberty, to wander uncontrolled in the air, like a wild bird, under green trees, among pleasant fruits, and sweet-smelling flowers.

'My quaint Ariel,' said Prospero to the little sprite when he made him free, 'I shall miss you; yet you shall have your freedom.'

'Thank you, my dear master,' said Ariel. 'But give me permission to look after your ship while it will travels towards your home. And after this job is done master, I shall live merrily!'

Prospero then buried deep in the earth his magical books and wand, for he was resolved never to make

use of the magic art. And having thus overcome his enemies, and being reconciled to his brother and the King of Naples, nothing now remained to complete his happiness, but to revisit his native land. The other things that would add to his happiness would be to take possession of his dukedom, and to witness the marriage of his daughter and Prince Ferdinand, which the King said should be instantly celebrated with great splendour on their return to Naples. And so, under the protective escort of the spirit Ariel, they, after a pleasant voyage, soon arrived at their homeland.

Glossary
Reconciled to be friendly again after estrangement
Splendour magnificent and brilliant

Post-reading Activities

Let's see if you remember

1. Who was Prospero and why did he cause the tempest in the sea?

2. Whom did Prospero live with and where?

3. Write short notes on the two servants of Prospero—Ariel and Caliban.

4. Make a character sketch of Miranda.

5. Name the people who landed on the island on which Miranda lived with her father.

6. Who was Ferdinand?

7. Why did Prospero want Ferdinand and Miranda to meet? Was he successful in his intention?

8. What was the task that Prospero gave Ferdinand in order to check his constancy?

9. Describe briefly the manner in which Prospero met his younger brother Antonio and the King?

10. From this incident what kind of a person do you think Prospero was?

11. What happens at the end of the story?

12. Do you think the title of the story is appropriate? Can you suggest another one?

About the Author

William Shakespeare was an English poet and playwright, universally acknowledged to be the greatest writer in English language. He is considered to be the world's pre-eminent dramatist also. He lived in the age of Queen Elizabeth I when England enjoyed a time of immense prosperity and stability. He is often called England's national poet and the 'Bard of Avon'.

It is indeed strange that though Shakespeare is recognized as one of literature's greatest influences, very little is actually known about him. Whatever we know about his life comes from the registrar records,

Glossary

Playwright a person who composes plays

court records, wills, marriage certificates and his tombstone.

Early Life

William Shakespeare was born in Stratford-on-Avon, the son of John Shakespeare, a glove maker and dealer in wool. John was a prominent man in Stratford. William's mother was Mary Arden who was the youngest daughter in her family. She inherited much of her father's landowning and farming estate when he died. William was the third child of John and Mary Shakespeare.

Shakespeare probably attended Stratford Grammar School in his childhood. When he was 18, he married Anne Hathaway in 1582. At that time Anne was 26, and already three months pregnant. After sometime his daughter, Susanna, was born. It is generally thought that he must have been in Stratford when Hamnet and Judith, his other two children were born in 1585.

Between the years 1580s and 1592, what Shakespeare did is unknown because no records of his life and works exist of that period. This period of time is often referred to as the 'lost years'. It is possible that he spent this entire period in London after leaving Stratford to escape a charge of deer poaching. Some records say that he was employed at a playhouse 'in a very mean Rank' during this time. Researchers make assumptions that during these 'lost years', Shakespeare might have tended horses for theatergoers or worked as a sailor, a teacher or a coachman. Some think that he might have been a soldier, a law clerk, a theater page, or a moneylender. He could have held several of these jobs or he may have held none of them!

Shakespeare may also have spent the time travelling to far off towns or even to foreign countries. His plays suggest that he visited Italy, for more than a dozen of them including *The Merchant of Venice, Romeo and Juliet, All's Well That Ends Well, Othello, Coriolanus, Julius Caesar, The Two Gentlemen of Verona, The Taming of the Shrew, Titus Andronicus, Much Ado About Nothing*, and *The Winter's Tale,* all have scenes set in Italy.

Career

How Shakespeare first started his career in the theatre no one knows for certain. Whether an acting troupe recruited Shakespeare in his hometown or he was forced on his own to travel to London to begin his career, is not clearly known. In the year 1592 came the first reference to Shakespeare in the world of theatre when Robert Greene an eminent writer of that time mentioned him in his writing. While in London, Shakespeare lived alone in rented accommodations while his wife and children remained in Stratford. Why his family did not move to London with him is unknown.

In 1592, when an epidemic of plague closed the theatres, the versatile Shakespeare wrote sonnets and other poetry until the theatres reopened in 1594. The same year, he joined a newly formed drama group called the 'Lord Chamberlain's Men', serving there as a writer and an actor.

Shakespeare produced most of his well-known works between 1589 and 1613. His early plays were mainly comedies and histories, the literary genre which he raised to the peak of artistic sophistication by the end of the 16th century. He then wrote mainly tragedies until about 1608, including *Hamlet, King Lear, Othello,* and *Macbeth,* all of which are considered to be the finest works in the English language. In the last

Glossary
Versatile able to adapt to many different functions or activities

years of his career, he wrote tragicomedies, also known as romances, and collaborated with other playwrights.

Shakespeare's works are the greatest representation of art from Elizabethan England. They encompass the economic, social, and educational aspects of life in a nice, neat package. No other art form, including painting, could provide so much information about life in Elizabethan England.

Theatre in Shakespeare's Times

During the age of Shakespeare, all plays which were written had to be approved by the government's censor. This is because plays at that time were considered morally or politically offensive and could be banned. It was considered so very offensive that many a time the playwright would be imprisoned too.

Shakespeare presented his plays at inns, courtyards, royal palaces, private residences, playhouses and the Globe Theatre built in 1599. The playhouses in Shakespeare's time were wooden structures with tiers of seating galleries in the shape of a horseshoe. They could seat two thousand to three thousand people who

Glossary
Imprisoned kept in prison in a captive state

paid two or more pennies. It is believed that at that time the theatre lovers who were wealthy could pay extra to sit on the stage! The main floor, which was surrounded by the galleries, had no roof and no seats. A person could stand and watch the play standing by paying a penny. This area was called a 'pit'. Up to one thousand people could stand and watch performances in this area under a hot sun or dark clouds.

The stage of the Globe theatre was four to six feet above ground level. There was no curtain that opened or closed at the beginning or at the end of the plays. A wall with two or three doors leading to the dressing rooms of the actors stood at the back of the stage. These rooms collectively were known as the 'tiring house'.

Males played all the characters, even that of women! Actors played gods, ghosts, demons, and other supernatural characters. They could pop up from the underworld through a trap door on the stage or descend down to Earth from heaven on a winch line from the ceiling. The sound of thunder was created off stage, by beating a sheet metal. To demonstrate that an actor had suffered a fencing wound, he simply had to slap his hand against a pouch beneath his shirt to release 'blood' showing his death.

Globe Theatre

Although Shakespeare's plays were performed at different venues during the playwright's career, the Globe Theatre in the Southwark district of London was the place at which his best known plays were first performed. The Globe was built during Shakespeare's early period in 1599 by one of his long-standing associates, Cuthbert Burbage.

The theater that Cuthbert Burbage built had a total capacity between 2,000 and 3,000 spectators. Due to the absence of electric lights, all performances at the Globe were conducted during the day (probably in the mid-afternoon spanning between 2 p.m. and 5 p.m.). As most of the stage of the Globe Theatre was open air and the apparatus for sound system were poor, the actors were compelled to shout their lines, stress their intonations, and engage themselves in exaggerated theatrical gestures. The plays which were staged at the Globe were completely devoid of background scenery

Glossary
Spectator a person who watches something—a show, a game, or any other event
Apparatus the equipment or machinery needed for a particular activity

although costumes and props were utilized. There was no proscenium arch, no curtains, and no stagehands than the actors themselves. Instead, changes of scenes were suggested in the speeches and narrative situations of the plays.

End of Globe Theatre

The original structure of the Globe Theatre existed until June 29, 1613, when its thatched roof was set on fire by a cannon fired during the performance of the play Henry VIII. The Globe burned to ashes and could not be saved. At this time, Shakespeare had almost retired and was at Stratford-on-Avon where he died three years later at the age of fifty-two. The Globe was reconstructed in the year 1614.

Glossary
Proscenium arch it is a kind of an arch which forms a framing on the opening between the stage and the auditorium in some theatres